Discovering
HILL FIGURES

Kate Bergamar

Shire Publications Ltd.

CONTENTS

Copyright © 1968 and 1986 by Kate Bergamar. Number 12 in the 'Discovering' series. ISBN 0 85263 798 5. First published 1968. Second edition 1972. Third edition 1986. All rights reserved. *No part of this publication may be reproduced or transmitted in any form or by any means without permission in writing from the publishers, Shire Publications Ltd, Cromwell House, Church Street, Princes Risborough, Aylesbury, Bucks HP17 9AJ, U.K.*

Printed by C. I. Thomas & Sons (Haverfordwest) Ltd, Press Buildings, Merlins Bridge, Haverfordwest, Dyfed.

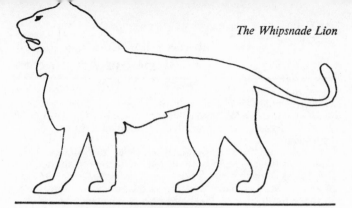

INTRODUCTION

The intaglio hill figures of England and Scotland are unique. Nearly all are worth visiting for their own sakes and the situation of many is so delightful that they form the perfect focus for summer expeditions and picnics.

We owe a great debt to those who maintain them: the Department of the Environment, the National Trust and other bodies, private owners or just public-spirited local people anxious to maintain a tradition. With the best care these figures are still vulnerable to thoughtless visitors who may walk on the fragile outlines and destroy them.

The best area for a tour is, of course, Wessex. All the figures in the region may be seen comfortably in a day or two, working in a leisurely fashion from a centre such as Marlborough or Avebury. As the contents list shows, isolated examples exist, too, in other counties. The best way to visit them is on foot along the downland tracks but even a confirmed motorist can plan a comprehensive tour. The Cerne Giant, the Long Man of Wilmington, the Chiltern Crosses and above all, the Uffington Horse, deserve visits of their own.

Mr. Gee's work on the Westbury horse in 1778, based perhaps on his knowledge of the Uffington prototype, inspired many imitators. Doctors, squires, farmers and rectors all planned adornments for their neighbourhoods. Many winter evenings must have passed agreeably with squared paper and compass, and summer days with flags, megaphones, spades and celebratory toasts at the end, around the new chalk figure, shining across the countryside. Despite the fine chalk slopes of Sussex and Bedfordshire, the idea never really caught on there, and it is in Wessex that they may be seen at their best and most dramatic.

3

Aberdeenshire (Grampian Region)
White Horse of Strichen

Location

Twelve miles N.W. of Peterhead, and $2\frac{1}{2}$ miles N.E. of Strichen, on the S.W. flank of Mormond Hill. On a slope of about 30 degrees: Mormond Hill is 769 feet high.

Approach

Travel south from Fraserburgh on A981 to Strichen. Mormond Hill lies to the left, about two miles before the village. The Horse is cut on the S.W. face. A track leading from the village to Brawns Farm and on to the ruined hunting lodge on the summit of the hill, passes near the Horse.

Best View

Mormond Hill dominates the Buchan Plain and the Horse is visible for a great distance from land and sea.

History

This is the only white horse in Scotland. Despite some doubts about its origin, all accounts attribute it to a member of the Fraser family, lairds of Strichen. One account says it was cut by Lord Strichen's grandson to commemorate a favourite white charger shot under him in battle. Another account mentions the Fraser who entertained Boswell and Johnson at Strichen in 1773, but as no mention is made of the Horse in the *Journal of a Tour of the Hebrides*, it appears to have been cut after this. The laird concerned is reputed to have been an eccentric who eventually died of frustration because he could not make the Horse's legs natural-looking enough! Another account attributes it to Lord Lovat. The general appearance of the Horse makes an eighteenth century date—the time of follies and pseudo-antiques—most likely, or perhaps one early in the nineteenth century.

The figure covers half an acre of ground and from nose to tail the horse is about 162 feet long. No chalk was available so the shape was filled with the white quartz stones of the neighbourhood. The eyeball is a mound of quartz 18 inches high. The horse is standing, with two legs shown in profile and only one ear.

Aberdeenshire (Grampian Region)
White Stag of Strichen

Location

Twelve miles N.W. of Peterhead, on the other side of Mormond Hill to the White Horse. Just above Whiteside Farm and facing S.E. on a shallow slope.

Approach
Leave Fraserburgh on the A92, travelling south. About half a mile after the fork junction with the A952, just before the road passes under the railway, turn right. The fifth farm road on the right leads to Whiteside Farm. The Stag is just above the farm.

Best View
From the approach road to the farm.

History
It was cut in 1870 by an architect, Mr. Gardner. The method used was the same as that for the Horse. The area of the body was filled with greyish limestone and quartz, giving a durable surface. It is a large figure, 240 feet long and covering nearly an acre. It is a striking piece of work, in the Balmoral Victorian tradition, and well deserves the care which has been given to it locally.

Bedfordshire

Whipsnade White Lion

Location
On the western face of the Dunstable Downs, immediately below Whipsnade Zoo Park, and about one mile north of the village of Dagnall.

Approach
Leave Berkhamsted on A41, turn right at Northchurch on B4506 and continue through to Dagnall village. About a mile after the village the Lion will be seen on the slope to the right.

Best View
From Ivinghoe Beacon and surrounding hills.

History
This chalk figure which greets all visitors to the Zoo was cut in 1935, from a design by R. B. Brook-Greaves. At first it was cut in outline only but later more chalk was removed and the whole animal became white. It measures 483 feet from nose to tail, its front legs measure 103 feet and the back legs 145 feet. The tail is 13 feet wide and the whole outline measures three-quarters of a mile. A concrete edging has now been provided to preserve the outline and weed-killers are used to combat grass and weeds. During the war it was camouflaged.

To commemorate the 50th anniversary of the Zoo, in 1981, the figure was outlined with 750 40 watt electric bulbs. It is illuminated on special occasions and this can also be sponsored by private individuals.

Inkpen Horse

Location
About six miles south of Hungerford on the west escarpment of Inkpen Beacon in the parish of Ham. The Horse has completely disappeared.

History
It is supposed to have been cut about 1868 by Mr. Wright who purchased Ham Spray House in the valley below, from which the Horse was designed to be seen. Mr. O. C. S. Crawford in 1922 noticed it marked on the six inch Ordnance Survey map of 1877. However Mr. Wright did not make a very thorough job of the cutting and merely stripped the turf away. The property was sold and in a short time the Horse became overgrown.

This would be an excellent site for future cutters, on a good slope of 35 degrees, which is visible for miles from the surrounding countryside.

Berkshire/Oxfordshire
Uffington White Horse

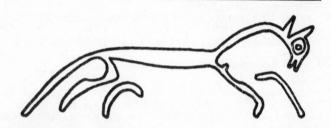

Location
A quarter of a mile N.E. of the Iron Age fort of Uffington Castle and two miles south of Uffington village. Just below the north escarpment of the Berkshire Downs, about five hundred feet above the Vale of the White Horse. The Horse faces N.W. on a slope of thirty degrees.

Approach
Travel westwards on B4507 Wantage-Swindon road. The sign to White Horse Hill will be seen on the left, immediately opposite the turn to Uffington village. Car park.

Best View

It can be seen from most points in the Vale from Swindon in the west almost to Abingdon in the east. The best view is probably from the Swindon-Reading railway line, four miles away, or from the air. It cannot be seen well from close quarters. On clear days, when freshly scoured, it is visible for 14-20 miles and the Rev. Francis Wise thought he could see it from Whiteleaf in Buckinghamshire.

History

Uffington White Horse is one of the most exciting monuments in Britain. It leaps fluidly across the sweeping curves of the downs; above are the high green ramparts of Uffington Castle and below the tree-butt form of Dragon's Hill. St. George is said to have slain the Dragon here: on the top where the Dragon's blood was spilt, grass has never grown. To the west the landscape is cut into a series of fantastic glacial terraces, known as the Giant's Stairs and the road up to the Castle sweeps across a deep combe called the Manger. Half a mile to the west is a prehistoric chambered barrow called Weland's Smithy, linked to the Castle by the Ridgeway. In front of the Horse lies the fertile patchwork of pasture and corn of the Vale and around is the short, sheep-trimmed grass of the Downs, with a profusion of wild flowers and larks.

Situated as it is amongst such dramatic surroundings it is not surprising to find that the Horse is surrounded by a web of mystery and conjecture. Very little is firmly known of its origins. It has provoked innumerable arguments and it has influenced the making of all the subsequent Wessex horses. But who made it? How? And why? These are still largely unanswered questions.

The first record of it was made in the reign of Henry II, when the Manor of Sparsholt was described as "near the place which is commonly called White Horse Hill". By the fourteenth century, the name Vale of the White Horse was established when a manuscript, now at Corpus Christi College, Cambridge, included the Horse as one of the wonders of Britain, second only to Stonehenge. By the seventeenth century the antiquaries' interest was aroused and the arguments had begun!

The Reverend Francis Wise was the first man to realise the importance of chalk figures as antiquities. His first description of the Horse in *A Letter to Dr. Mead concerning some Antiquities in Berkshire,* 1738, shows that little change has taken place in 230 years. His comment, "the horse at first view is enough to raise the admiration of every curious

spectator", is still perfectly valid. The early antiquaries des-
pised the Horse as a piece of 'rude' and 'barbarous' work.
Some resolved their dislike by showing it as a stolid Georgian
animal in their engravings. In fact the Horse is curiously
modern in appearance and far more in tune with twentieth
century taste than the horses cut later. It is a piece of pure art.

Aubrey, the seventeenth century antiquary, said that,
"the White Horse was made by Hengist, who bore one on his
arms". Another favourite theory is that Alfred (born nearby
at Wantage) had it cut as a memorial to his victory over the
Danes in A.D. 871 but there is no evidence for this. It is true
that a prancing horse was a Saxon symbol, although their
horse was on its hind legs and facing left, while the Uffington
Horse gallops to the right. In his *Ballad of the White Horse*,
Chesterton makes Alfred scour a far older horse, rather than
create a new one:

> 'Before the gods that made the gods,
> Had seen their sunrise pass,
> The White Horse of the White Horse Vale,
> Was cut out of the grass'.

There is no evidence to support this poetic licence, although
the poem does express the atmosphere of the area.

The Department of the Environment, in its official list,
stated that it was probably made by the Belgae. It is in
the non-representational tradition of Celtic art and they mention a strong resemblance to the stylized horses on the reverse
of Celtic imitations of the gold staters of Philip of Macedon.
These coins were first imported from Gaul but were later
struck in Britain with a design of horses with beaked heads
and disjointed bodies, facing right. Two horses, strongly
reminiscent of the Uffington Horse, appear on *répoussé*
buckets, one from Marlborough (now in Devizes Museum),
and the other from Aylesford (now in the British Museum).
It is possible that the figure was cut late in the first century
B.C.

The Horse was obviously meant to be seen from a distance.
It seems most likely that it was a cult-figure or tribal symbol
for the people of the neighbourhood and was linked in some
way with the Castle, for the festivities held within the ramparts
during the scouring point to this. There is much evidence of
animal worship in the Iron Age and the horse symbol occurs
over and over again. In appearance the Uffington figure is not
much like a horse. Many have preferred to call it a dragon
and link it with Dragon's Hill. It is about 360 feet long (and
so the largest of the white horses). A single flowing line runs
from nose to tail. Two legs are joined to the body and two are

free, its head is beaked, with a deep cleft between the ears and the eye is large and round, at present about four feet in diameter. Despite its dragon-like appearance it has now been known as a horse for nearly 900 years so the tradition is very firmly established.

Legends

A local tradition says that the Horse is slowly moving uphill. The official photographs do show shadowy lines beneath the present outline but there seems little reason to think that its shape has changed much since it was first cut.

Another tradition is that the shoes for the Horse are made by Weland at his Smithy half a mile away: in the Scandinavian legend Weland actually owned a white horse himself. This service was available for any traveller in need, who cared to tie his horse up at the entrance, place a groat on the capstone and go away. On his return the work would have been done.

Another local belief is that to stand on the Horse's eye with closed eyes, to turn round three times and to wish, will bring good luck.

The Scouring or 'Pastime'

The scouring of the Horse took place every seven years, a mystical number in itself. It had all the qualities of a pagan festival. While the actual work was in progress, a 'pastime' was held within the ramparts of the Castle, with sports and a fair. Thomas Hughes, in his novel *The Scouring of the White Horse*, describes the scouring ceremony in 1857, and some of the associated amusements, and Francis Wise, writing in 1738, remarked that it was a very old custom to hold the ceremony. People assembled from all the surrounding villages, which shared the duty of keeping the Horse clean. The obligation to undertake this was one of the conditions upon which the Lord of the Manor held his land and he was also obliged to feed and entertain the diggers!

The pastime lasted two days. Booths and sideshows were set up and the usual crowd of pickpockets, pedlars and showmen assembled. In 1843 Wombwell's Circus attended and had great difficulty in getting the elephant's van up the downland track. Races were held for horses, asses and men in sacks; the ladies raced for smocks (the second prize a silk hat), and cheeses were bowled down the Manger. The Town Crier of Wantage announced the events and plenty of cakes and ale were available for the diggers. During the actual scouring a ballad in Berkshire dialect was sung:

> The owl White Horse wants zetting to rights,
> And the Squire hev promised good cheer,

Zo we'll gee un a scrape to kip un in shape,
And a'll last for many a year!

The pastime seems to have lapsed after 1857 and even the scouring was done irregularly. By 1880 the horse was so overgrown as to be practically invisible to those not knowing its whereabouts, but four years later it was cleaned and recut. Lady Craven paid for the next scouring in 1892, but when the British Association visited the Horse in 1894 it was again weed-grown. Now the Horse, Castle and Weland's Smithy are all expertly cared for by English Heritage.

Buckinghamshire
Bledlow Cross

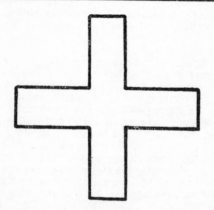

Location
In the Chilterns, on the N.W. face of Wain Hill, just below the crest. About one mile east of Chinnor village and on the 500 foot contour line.

Approach
Leave Chinnor on the B4009, in the direction of Aylesbury. About one mile from the village a track leads right signposted "Wain Hill only". This crosses the old Watlington-Princes Risborough railway line. Cars may not pass the letter box, but continue on foot up to a modern house with a white front door. Turn up the path to the left of the Chinnor Hill Nature Reserve board, for about 200 yards. The Cross is to the left of this path.

Best View

From the Henton turn on the B4009, about a mile from Chinnor in the Aylesbury direction.

History

Its origin, like that of the Whiteleaf Cross, four miles away, is uncertain. Some experts think that the nearness of both Crosses to the Icknield Way, which passes just below them, indicates a connection with travellers and direction finding. Even in a good state, however, the Bledlow Cross is not visible from all directions.

In volume VII of the Records of Bucks, E. J. Payne suggested that the Crosses were military beacons made during the Civil War but this is hardly a serious theory. Some experts think that the Crosses started as phallic symbols, similar to the Watlington White Mark, and were later Christianized.

Two pieces of evidence point to the Bledlow Cross having been cut later than 1757. A letter from Stukeley's correspondence of that date clearly mentions the Whiteleaf Cross, but ignores that at Bledlow. The small size of the cross described by Lipscomb suggests an eighteenth-century origin, for chalk figures tend to increase in size with each scouring. It is now about 73 feet across and the arms are 12 feet wide. In 1847 Lipscomb commented that it was 'much obscured by grass and weeds, being only at distant intervals retraced'.

Buckinghamshire
Whiteleaf Cross

Location

On a steep slope of the Chilterns, on a slope of 25-45 degrees, facing west over the Vale of Aylesbury, near Monks Risborough. The Icknield Way passes below it. It can be seen from Headington Hill, Oxford, and the Rev. Francis Wise felt sure he could see it from Uffington Castle, thirty miles away.

Approach

Leave Princes Risborough on the A4010, travelling towards Aylesbury. Turn right at Peters Lane, Monks Risborough. Continue to the car park and picnic site and walk along the Ridgeway Path to the top of the Cross.

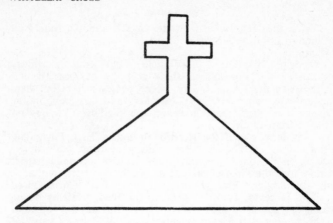

Best View

From many points in the western Vale of Aylesbury. Especially good from a point about 200 yards short of the junction of the B4009 with A4129 Thame to Princes Risborough road. It can also been seen from the Henton turn on B4009, near Chinnor, the view point for the Bledlow Cross.

History

Once again the origins are obscure. H. J. Massingham made a wild guess in his book *Chiltern Country* and equated it with the Uffington Horse, the Long Man of Wilmington and the Cerne Giant, in date. To him Whiteleaf Cross was an astrological or phallic monument of the Bronze Age. Wise saw it as a possible site of a Saxon victory over the Danes.

An attractive theory is to make it the work of the monks of Monks Risborough (if indeed they really lived in the village; many believe they merely held the manor) or Great Missenden, five miles away. There seems a lot to be said for their having constructed the Cross as a devotional and practical monument for travellers, in the way that any other roadside cross was made.

In a charter of A.D. 903, reference is made to a boundary mark in the vicinity of Whiteleaf, known as Wayland's Stock, approached by a paved way. This was a phallic symbol and was perhaps later reshaped by the monks into the Cross.

Over the years considerable difference in the measurements of this Latin Cross have been recorded. It now is about 80 feet across, with arms 20 feet wide. Apparently the size has increased in the past 200 years. The engraving in Wise's *Further Observations on the White Horse, 1742*, shows a far slimmer and more shapely figure. Weathering is severe and was aggravated in the nineteenth century by visitors, who amused themselves by sliding down the shaft on faggots. In some places the chalk surface is deeply below the surface of the turf. Locally the base has always been known as the 'globe'.

Scouring

This seems to have been a festive occasion. Lipscomb in 1847 mentions it as a local custom and says that the local people believed that at one time the Oxford Colleges had taken a hand in it but "it is now borne by the neighbourhood, and never without a merry-making".

In 1826 George Robert, Earl of Buckinghamshire, succeeded to the Hampden estate and had the turf round the Cross renewed and the outlines recut. In 1935 five acres of surrounding land were vested in the National Trust to safeguard the view from the Cross, which now appears on the official list of ancient monuments. Scouring is now the responsibility of the Bucks County Council and the Cross is currently in good condition.

Cambridgeshire
Gogmagog Giants

Location

On the ramparts of Wandlebury Camp, south of Cambridge. They have now completely disappeared.

History

The earliest reference to the figures was in *Mundus alter et idem* by Joseph Hall, published in Frankfurt in 1605. Hall was a Cambridge graduate. A legend associated the cutting with the Vandal prisoners transferred to this country by the Emperor Probus to reinforce the army. An earlier chronicler says they built Wandlebury Camp (Vandalsburgh). If this guess is at all correct the giants dated from about A.D. 300.

Another account firmly attributes the giants to the work of undergraduates. The group lay on the rampart and John Layer, in 1640, wrote of 'a high and mighty figure of a giant which the scholars of Cambridge cut upon the turf'. As the giant appeared on the rampart it cannot have been large and could conceivably have been the work of one summer's day.

If so, the undergraduates were merely adding to a legend for in 1200 the hill was associated with a giant, who gave it the name Gogmagog. They merely added a portrait to the myth. Now nothing can be seen for the site was destroyed when Lord Godolphin made his garden there in the eighteenth century and it had disappeared by 1800.

Several years ago T. C. Lethbridge announced further discoveries. By a combination of excavation and probing he found a group of giants representing the Sun Chariot, the God of Darkness and the Moon Goddess and further research is now necessary to clarify this new find.

Devon
Plymouth Giants

Location

On Plymouth Hoe. Not visible today.

History

Though these giants have now vanished, they are well documented. The Plymouth Corporation audit book gives various entries about the maintenance of the first giant:

    1529–30.   Cleansing of Gog Magog 8d.
    1566–7.   20d new cutting the Gogmagog.

Some feel that two giants existed or that confusion may have arisen from the division of the name into two, Gog and Magog, at the London Guildhall, and that at Plymouth, in the first instance, only one giant existed.

But by 1602 when Carew's *Survey of Cornwall* was published there were two. 'Upon the Haw at Plymouth there is cut in the ground the portrayture of two men, the one bigger, the one lesser, with clubbes in their handes . . . it is renewed by order of the Townsmen when cause requireth. . . .' The second giant became known as Corineus, the giant of Cornwall, who fought Gogmagog in a classic battle.

The figures were certainly cut out of the turf on the steeply sloping part probably near Goemagot's Leap, where Corineus is supposed to have thrown Gogmagog into the sea. They appear to have been visible in 1750 and perhaps for some years after that.

Dorset
Cerne Giant

Location

On Giant Hill, a quarter of a mile N.W. of Cerne Abbas and eight miles north of Dorchester, just east of A352. The figure faces west.

Approach

Leave Dorchester and travel north on the A352 to Cerne Abbas. After the sharp bend in the middle of the village a side road to the right leads up to Giant Hill. A footpath continues up to the figure.

Best View

It can be seen from various points in the village. The best view is west of the main road, A352, which the figure overlooks. A good view, too, is from the other side of the valley.

Appearance

The figure is about 180 feet high and 45 feet across the shoulders. The head is about 24 feet and the eye three feet in diameter. The club is 120 feet long. Its size has not changed since it was surveyed in the eighteenth century. The outline trench is about two feet wide and altogether 480 yards of trenching are involved in the outline.

The figure is of a nude man, with ribs, phallus and nipples accentuated. One writer called it the 'most remarkable portrait in Britain of male aggressiveness and sexual energy' and the *Gentleman's Magazine* of 1764 added, in awed tones, that its club was raised to strike a blow 'sufficient to overturn a mountain'.

History

Behind the Giant is a rectangular enclosure known locally as the Frying Pan or Trendle and this for centuries was the scene of maypole celebrations at Midsummer. Such a ceremony held within yards of the Giant seems to point to some dim folk recollection of a fertility rite.

One legend says that the people of Cerne drew the figure of the Giant round the body of a real giant, whom they killed as he lay on the hillside sleeping off a heavy meal of sheep. Another legend makes him a devourer of maidens and a third maintains that a girl who sleeps on the Giant will be the mother of many children. The fertility association is strong, for childless couples are still known to visit the Giant and these beliefs may be the key to his original role in the life of the community.

Cerne, according to William of Malmesbury, was the home of a particularly stubborn brand of paganism.

Since the Giant is so near the Abbey attempts have been made to connect it with the monks. Some have thought it a monkish joke, made at the Dissolution, about the habits of the Abbot. If the monks did not make the Giant, they did not interfere with it. Why did they not destroy so blatantly pagan an object? Clearly the reason must have been both effective and powerful.

Perhaps a belief in its usefulness lingered on. It is recorded that in 1268 the monks of Lanercost obligingly made a fertility figure of Priapus for the local people, whose cattle were diseased, so religious houses were not completely unsympathetic to earlier beliefs. Hutchins, in his *History of Dorset* 1774, mentions the date 798 and vague symbols which could be the Christian symbols IHS, between the Giant's knees, and these could have been a token attempt to Christianize the figure. Again, by the church is a holy well, made by St. Augustine, and Cerne Women's Institute in their history of the village quote the local formula 'with your back to the Giant, you should make a cup of a laurel leaf and wish facing the Church' which again may be an attempt to encourage a shift of focus from Giant to Church.

In 1764 Stukeley made the sensible guess that the figure might represent Hercules and the National Trust, in their official handbook, agrees with this view. The club and other attributes reinforce this theory, for the somewhat wooden form is typical of Romano-British art and examples of similar figures can be found on the pottery and altars of the period. A revival of the Hercules cult took place at the end of the second century A.D.

So it appears that for nearly two thousand years the Giant has been an important influence in Cerne Abbas, at first as promoter of fertility in wives, herds and flocks and more lately as a tourist attraction and as an object of a certain reverence and affection.

Scouring

The scouring has always been faithfully attended to by local people. Once again seven years seems to have been the usual interval between scourings. Hutchins has a story that the figure was cut by the tenants of Lord Holles, who lived near Cerne, but this cannot be substantiated and may be merely a recollection of a scouring. However, as with some other figures there is always a faint possibility that the Giant may be the work of a Georgian squire with a Rabelaisian taste for the antique. In 1920 the figure was presented to the National Trust by Mr. G. Pitt-Rivers and was later endowed by Sir

Henry Hoare of Stourhead. It is thus kept in excellent condition today. The scouring takes four men a full day.

Dorset
Osmington Horse

Location

Three and a half miles N.W. of Weymouth, near Osmington village, facing south over Weymouth Bay.

Approach

Leave Weymouth on A353, travelling east. About three miles out of the town take the left turn to Sutton Poyntz. Fork right in the village. At the end of this road a footpath leads up to the Horse.

Best View

From Weymouth Bay, or from the A353 between Preston and Osmington.

History

Several different stories are told about its cutting. One attributes it to a soldier stationed in the area in the early nineteenth century, who cut it to commemorate the visits that George III and his brother the Duke of Gloucester paid to Weymouth, from 1789. This could be correct because undoubtedly Weymouth owed a good deal of its prosperity to these visits but the figure could hardly be the work of one man. It covers nearly an acre!

Another version makes it the work of a group of engineers, stationed in Weymouth when fear of a Napoleonic invasion was at its height. To engineers the work would be easy and no doubt they had plenty of free time during the waiting period. Thomas Hardy put forward yet another view, in *The Trumpet Major,* that it commemorated the Battle of Trafalgar.

It is tempting to think that the cutting may have been prompted by the town. It was extremely conscious of the value of the King's visits and a massive statue to him was erected on the esplanade. The bathing women of Weymouth had 'God Save the King' embroidered on their belts and whenever the King entered the water a band struck up the national anthem! The white horses of Hanover were seen all over the town.

The Dorset Official Guide, issued by authority of the County Council, says that the 260 foot long Horse had already been cut in 1807 and that the figure of the King was added as a gesture of appreciation for royal visits. They say that the King was highly offended by the fact that he appeared to be riding away from Weymouth and felt himself insulted. He never visited the town again.

The Horse has the distinction of being the only one to carry a rider. The pose reminds one of many public statues: one foreleg is raised, the head is finely modelled and all four reins are shown. The somewhat unimpressive rider holds a stick and his spurred foot shows oddly beneath the line of the Horse's belly. The tail is long and graceful and the figure is 280 feet long, placing it second in size only to the Uffington Horse.

Scouring

Although there have been arguments about the scouring the work has always been done somehow. In 1928 twelve unemployed men were set to work by the Weymouth Chamber of Commerce at a cost of £40. Later Boy scouts and voluntary labour have dealt with it.

Hampshire
Woolbury Horse

Location

On the southern rampart of Woolbury Camp, two miles east of Stockbridge.

Approach

Leave Stockbridge on the A272 in the direction of Winchester. About a mile out of the town a footpath on the left leads up to the Camp. This path leaves the road almost opposite the side road to Little Somborne.

Best View

The figure is so small that the best view is really from the camp itself.

History

Its date and origin are unknown. The construction is crude and the outline largely of rough flints, pressed into the ground. It was about 27 feet long when last measured and the tail was made of a line of flints. However the construction was frail and could very easily be destroyed. In 1929 the landowner repaired and whitewashed it, but its existence has always been precarious.

Only one printed reference is known which appeared in *Notes and Queries* for November, 1859, so it at least dates from the mid-nineteenth century. A local legend associates it with a copse on the main Winchester road, known as Robber's Roost which is supposed to have been the refuge of a highwayman who waylaid the Winchester to Salisbury coaches. The Woolbury Horse is said to be a portrait of his mount. This suggests that the Horse may be eighteenth century in origin.

The Horse lies just outside the Stockbridge Down National Trust property. It was remade in 1967 by the Stockbridge Youth Club.

Buffs Badge, Canterbury

Location
It has now gone but was cut on a turf bank at the end of the open air 300 yards range, in Military Road, Canterbury.
History
It was cut in 1922 by C.S.M. Oliver Mason of The Buffs. In its heyday it was the most notable badge outside Wessex and was 51 feet long and was, of course, a dragon, the regimental badge of The Buffs.

Col. H. R. Grace kindly told me that in 1958 all Regimental Depots were abolished and more drastically, in 1961, The Buffs were amalgamated with The Queen's Own Royal West Kent Regiment. Sadly, the Dragon did not exist after 1958.

Kent

Wye Crown

Location
One mile S.E. of Wye, on the North Downs.
Approach
Leave Ashford on the A28 Canterbury road. In three miles turn right for Wye village. Go through the village in the direction of Hastingleigh. About a mile from Wye the Crown will be seen on the escarpment to the left, above Coldharbour Farm. A footpath leads up to it.
Best View
Visible over a wide area as the ground is flat in this neighbourhood. The best view is probably from about three miles beyond Ashford, from the Ashford to Canterbury road, or from the air.
History
This is the only example of a chalk crown and is 240 feet wide. The outline trench is 12 feet wide. The crown is now the property of Wye College. An article about the

history of the Crown by Dr. H. H. Glasscock appeared in the College Old Students' Journal, Vol. VI No. 2, 1965 and he has kindly allowed me to draw on the facts that appear in it. It was designed in 1902 by T. J. Young, who was Lecturer in Agriculture and later Vice-Principal of the College. First attempts to peg it out ran into difficulties. A unique method of construction was then devised and a paper shape of a design taken from a coin of the realm was stuck to the object lens of a theodolite. The instrument was sited near Withersdane Farm and students, directed by hand signals, placed flags round the outline. An official of the Royal Mint suggests that the 1887 florin was the coin used in the design.

The Crown was illuminated in August, 1902, for the Coronation of King Edward VII, for which occasion it was cut. It was lighted by 1,500 fairy lamps which had been hung on notched sticks the day before by boys from Wye School. It is said that the Crown could be seen from Hastings to Tenterden: one of the most dramatic illuminations in the country. Fireworks added to the display. The Crown has been illuminated on other occasions and in 1935 fifteen hundred 25 watt electric light bulbs were used for the first time to mark the Jubilee of King George V. The night was clear and warm and once again the Crown could be seen from Hastings.

The Crown is now maintained by the Students' Union Society who make up working parties whenever cleaning is required. During the Guy Fawkes festivities each year a procession of lighted torches from the College to Coldharbour Farm takes place and finishes at the Crown with a firework display.

Oxfordshire
Watlington White Mark

Location

On Watlington Hill, part of the Chiltern escarpment on which Bledlow Cross is cut a few miles away. The Mark is on the western face at about the 500 foot contour line and points up towards Christmas Common.

Approach

Leave Stokenchurch on the A40 in the direction of Oxford and turn left at the Lambert Arms, about three miles from Stokenchurch. In Watlington, four miles on, turn left along Hill Road for Christmas Common. The Mark will be seen on the right about a mile out of the town.

Best View
From the road between Watlington and Christmas Common, at a point just after the Hospital (the viewpoint from which the photograph was taken).

History
Some authorities think that the Mark is a phallic symbol and that the Whiteleaf and Bledlow Crosses looked like this before Christianizing. The White Mark, however, seems to have been cut by Edward Horne in 1764, as an elegant obelisk and estate ornament. Watlington Hill is now a National Trust property.

Sussex
Ditchling Cross

Location
Cut in the turf of the South Downs above Plumpton Place, about five miles N.W. of Lewes.

Approach
Leaves Lewes on A275, travelling north. Turn left about a mile outside the town on B2116 for Plumpton. The Cross will be seen above Plumpton Place.

Best View
In good conditions it can be seen from the north for a considerable distance.

History
The Cross seems to be connected with the Battle of Lewes which was fought round the nearby hill called Mount Harry in May, 1264. Simon de Montfort defeated Henry III and the Cross may have been cut by the monks of Southover to remind travellers to pray for the souls of the fallen. It must have been made some time after the battle, although nothing is known of the date. In 1924 a monument was placed in the centre of the Cross, on the 660th anniversary of the Battle, but was destroyed in 1977.

The Cross was of the Greek type, 100 feet across, but is no longer visible.

Sussex
Litlington Horse

Location
On Hindover Hill, S.W. of Litlington village and three and a half miles from Seaford.

Approach
Leave Seaford on the A259, fork left at Sutton on to the

B2108. About two miles from the junction Hindover Hill will be seen to the right, between the road and Cuckmere River.

Best View

From the higher parts of Beachy Head and from the sea off Cuckmere Haven. A good view can be obtained, too, from the opposite side of the valley, near Charlston.

History

There have been two horses on this site. The older, now vanished, was supposed to have been cut in a single day in 1838 to mark the Coronation of Queen Victoria. In her *History of Alfriston,* Florence A. Pagden says that the party consisted of her father, James Pagden of Frog Firle, and her brothers, although the Town Guide of 1965 says that in 1860 two youths saw a patch of chalk resembling a horse's head and added the rest of the body. The first story seems the more likely.

The existing Horse was probably cut in February 1924 by John T. Ade and two friends, working by moonlight. John Ade's grandfather, William Ade, helped the Pagdens cut the original figure. It is slightly south-east of the supposed position of the first horse. It is standing and is about 90 feet long. In the 1930s it was neglected but it was thoroughly restored after 1945 by Air Ministry contractors.

Legend

There seems to be a local legend that the Horse was a monument to a girl whose horse bolted down this hill, throwing and killing her.

Sussex

Long Man of Wilmington

Location

On the north face of Windover Hill, three miles north of Eastbourne, and one mile south of the main Hastings-Lewes road. Faces slightly E. of N. on the steep slope, behind the village of Wilmington. It is on the best possible site, on a slope of forty degrees. The head is 500 feet above sea-level.

Approach

From Eastbourne take the main road north to Polegate forking left just before the railway bridge north of Polegate. Continue for about three miles along this road to Wilmington. If Wilmington Priory is also visited, turn right after leaving the front gate. The footpath to the figure leaves the main road at the second field gate on the left and the walk from the Priory takes about fifteen minutes.

Best View

From the road a little beyond the Priory entrance.

History

Absolutely nothing is known of the history of the Long Man (which has also been known in the past as the Lone Man, the Lanky Man or, when overgrown, the Green Man). The figure is slim and athletic, quite unlike the muscle-bound Cerne Giant. Little attempt at detail has been made but the figure holds two staffs, one on either side.

Its present appearance dates only from 1873 when the Duke of Devonshire paid for restoration and the figure was outlined with yellow bricks. In 1925 Wilmington Priory and the Long Man were conveyed to the Sussex Archaeological Society by the ninth Duke of Devonshire and the Society now arranges for repairs to the figure and white-washing.

The figure is 231 feet high and the staffs are 231 feet and 235 feet high and 115 feet apart. The shape is well designed to reduce foreshortening and the feet are shown in perspective so one can assume that it was pegged out under instructions from a distance. It is said to be the largest representation of the human figure in the world.

The earliest account of the Man is in a Burrell MS of 1779, now in the British Museum, and in this the Long Man holds a rake and scythe. There is a local tradition that the Man once wore a cap but this seems to be merely confusion with the local rhyme:

> When Firle or Long Man wears a cap,
> We in the valley gets a drap.

In other words, when clouds cover the Long Man's head they are lower than 500 feet and rain follows.

Very many fanciful theories have been put forward about the figure's identity. It has been seen as Mercury, Mohammed, St. Paul, a Roman soldier or a Saxon haymaker. A local legend says that two giants lived on Windover Hill and Firle Beacon, and that they quarrelled. Stones were thrown and Windover giant was killed; he lies where he fell. Flinders Petrie saw him as the Hindu deity Varuna, opening the gates of Heaven. Other archaeologists suggested that the figure was of a Roman soldier in the classic pose of the coins of the fourth century A.D., holding a standard in either hand. Another authority felt it might be the work of Roman soldiers with time on their hands. It is astonishing that so many chalk figures have been attributed to idle moments, although in fact the work of cutting them is gruelling to a degree and highly unsuitable as a pastime for the idle. The local press reported that Roman bricks had been found during the work of 1873.

The bricks were replaced with concrete blocks in 1969. Resistivity tests are said to have shown that the Long Man may have held a rake in one hand and a scythe in the other, with a plume in his hair.

In the neighbourhood it is said that a figure of a cock could be seen to the right of the figure until about 1870 and this gave rise to the theories involving St. Paul and Mohammed, whose symbols included a cock. King Harold of the Saxons used a device of a 'fighting man' on his arms and the figure may represent him holding a spear in either hand.

Until 1414 a Benedictine priory existed at Wilmington and at one time the Man was considered to be the work of the monks. If a monk made it, it was a monk with a purpose and the figure is so lacking in sex that any association with fertility figures such as the Cerne Giant can be dismissed at once.

The Sussex Archaeological Society feels that there is no connection between the figure and the Priory but other experts feel that it is just possible that it was made as a landmark, perhaps in the same way as the Whiteleaf Cross. There seems to be some confused local association between pilgrim traffic and the Long Man for a folk-tale of the neighbourhood tells of a giant killed by pilgrims on their way to Wilmington.

On balance, the most promising theories, which at best are only guesses, seem to be of a representation of Harold's Fighting Man or of a landmark associated in some way with the Priory. There is a slight possibility too, as with other figures, that it could be the work of an eighteenth century squire but when Burrell wrote in 1779 he knew nothing of its origins, so it cannot have been recently made. There is a strong resemblance between the Long Man and the figures on the Sutton Hoo designs and on a gold buckle found in a Saxon cemetery at Finglesham, Kent, so its origins could very well be Saxon with later modifications.

Warwickshire

Red Horse of Tysoe

Location

No trace can now be seen of the Horse but it was eight miles from Banbury, where the Banbury-Stratford-upon-Avon road descends the Edgehill escarpment near Lower, or Temple Tysoe and overlooking the village.

Approach

Leave Banbury on the A422 to Stratford. The road descends the escarpment at Sun Rising Inn (still to be seen though no longer an inn): the site of the second Horse was on

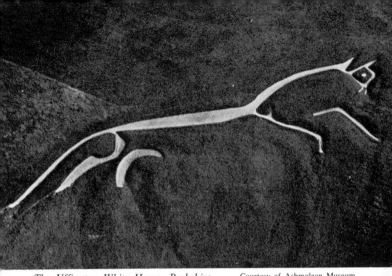

The Uffington White Horse, Berkshire   Courtesy of Ashmolean Museum

The Uffington Horse as engraved for 'The Modern British Traveller' (c.1750)

The Whiteleaf Cross, Bucks as depicted on a local inn sign.

Cadbury Lamb

The Watlington White Mark, Oxfordshire

Mary Farnell

The Long Man, Wilmington, Sussex

Harry C. Deal

The Wye Crown, Kent (by courtesy of Wye College Library)

The Red Horse of Tysoe. A wash drawing from the Aylesford Collection. (Birmingham Reference Library, Local History Dept.)

Laverstock Panda, Wiltshire   Press Association

Cherhill Horse, Wiltshire

David Uttley

Marlborough Horse, Wiltshire

David Uttley

The Bulford Kiwi, Wiltshire, undergoing scouring.

Ministry of Defence

Osmington Horse, Dorset.

Cadbury Lamb

Alton Barnes Horse, Wiltshire

New Pewsey Horse, Wiltshire

Regimental badges at Fovant, Wiltshire

a hill near the inn. The earlier Horse overlooked the village of Lower Tysoe for which. turn left a half mile after passing the Sun Rising Inn.

History

I am greatly indebted to Mr. Kenneth Carrdus of Banbury for these notes on the Red Horse. In recent years Mr. Carrdus, who is joint-author of *The Red Horse of Tysoe*, 1965, has, with Mr. W. G. Miller, done much valuable research on the figure's complicated history, making it possibly the best documented hill figure in England in an authoritative and scientific way.

The place-name Tysoe means 'spur of land dedicated to the god Tiu'—the Germanic Mars, and the reddish-brown soil of Edgehill is most suitable for an effigy in honour of the war-god. The Angles who colonized the Stour valley in the sixth century were members of a horse cult and cut a horse figure 200 feet long and 250 feet high, with (since it was a fertility symbol) the front half of a foal galloping in front of its mother. As a piece of Spring solstice magic they scoured the figure, sacrificed horses and ate the flesh and while, with the conversion to Christianity, the sacrificial meal was suppressed, farmers continued to scour the Horse on Palm Sunday for a thousand years.

Camden first recorded the Horse in his *Britannia*, 1607: 'Of the redy soil here come the names of Rodway and Rodley; yea and a great part of the very vale is there upon termed the vale of Red-horse, of the shape of an horse cut out in a red hill by the country people hard by Pillerton'. Dugdale perhaps saw the Horse at the battle of Edgehill and in the *Antiquities of Warwickshire*, 1656, wrote: 'there is cut upon the side of Edgehill the proportion of a horse in a very large form. The trenches of which ground, where the shape of the said horse is so cut out, being yearly scoured by a free-holder in this Lordship (of Tysoe), who holds certain lands there by that service'. This refers to modern Dinsdale Farm in Upper Tysoe, once Red Horse Farm.

In 1727 Beighton marked the Horse on his map of Warwickshire, showing it due east of Tysoe church. Since it faced right this could only mean that the great Saxon horse (which faced left) had been allowed to grass over and a much smaller figure, only 55 feet long, had been made above the Foal. The Reverend Francis Wise visited the Horse about 1740 in a critical mood, annoyed by the Vicar of Banbury's satirical comments on Wise's pamphlet on the Uffington Horse and other antiquities, and compared the two figures, to the demerit of the Red Horse; 'it is vastly inferior in every

33

respect . . . in its design, dimensions, fabrick and situation; being hardly visible at a distance. The whole betrays itself to be the work of a later age, and more rude workmen.' By 1767 the Horse was to be immortalized in Jago's poem *Edgehill:*

> 'Studious to preserve
> The fav'rite form, the treach'rous conquerors,
> Their vassal tribes compel, with festive rites,
> Its fading figure yearly to renew . . . '

Before the enclosures of 1800 the surveyor Godson marked the exact position of the Red Horse on a map, now in possession of the Marquess of Northampton, and Richard Gough measured it precisely (the eye, for instance, was one foot and two inches in diameter) and published these measurements in his edition of Camden's *Britannia,* 1806. After this the second, smaller figure was allowed to grass over, and the landlord of the Sun Rising Inn cut another still smaller figure, 17 feet long, on the hillside below his inn. This inn-sign lasted until about 1914 and the site is now overgrown with trees.

In 1959 Lord Bearsted afforested the Edgehill slopes, including Red Horse Hill and all chance of recovering the figure appeared lost, until in the dry summer of 1964 Graham Miller discovered a crop mark outline from a ground photograph. In the following spring Kenneth Carrdus made an aerial survey and from these photographs it has been possible to sketch the precise outlines of the Saxon horse and foal, and of the smaller eighteen century figure. A resistivity survey made by Dr. Stanley confirmed that the crop mark was caused by some deep, man-made disturbance, and excavations on the top ear in 1969 revealed that the Horse was cut into the clay at a depth of 2 feet 6 inches and was a solid figure, outlined by a narrow trench about 6 inches deeper. Further tests are being made, in the hope of proving the date of the original cutting, A.D. 600, and it is possible that permission may be given for the figure to be re-cut. If so, the largest Saxon work of art in England will again be seen and the Stour Valley from Edgehill to Stratford-upon-Avon can once again be called the Vale of the Red Horse.

Wiltshire
Alton Barnes Horse

Location

About one mile north of the village of Alton Barnes, near the long barrow known as Adam's Grave, about 650 feet above sea-level and 250 feet above the Vale of Pewsey. The slope is only thirty degrees and not really steep enough. However, the Horse is supposed to be visible from Old Sarum, 22 miles away. The Horse lies in a wide shallow dip between Walkers Hill and Milk Hill and is in the centre of a group of tumuli and barrows.

Approach

Leave Devizes on A361, Swindon road. Two miles out of the town turn right to Horton, Allington and Alton Barnes. In Alton Barnes turn left. In about one mile Walkers Hill will be seen on the left, with Adam's Grave and the Horse.

Best View

From the Canal Bridge, over the Kennett and Avon Canal, one mile south of the Horse. Also good from the road beneath the downs, between Alton Barnes and Stanton St. Bernard.

History

In 1868 the Reverend E. H. M. Sladen, formerly Rector of Alton Barnes, wrote that the Horse had been cut in 1812 by a farmer of Alton Barnes, Robert Pile of the Manor Farm. This man was also the creator of the Pewsey Old Horse (unless, as some think, the Alton Barnes Horse was made by his son, of the same name). An artist, known as Jack the Painter, whose real name was John Thorne, was chosen to design and cut the figure on the wide hill above the village. Unfortunately Mr. Pile's choice of workman was unlucky. For £20, paid in advance, Jack agreed to excavate the Horse to a depth of one foot and to fill up the cavity with chalk. In the event he employed John Harvey of Stanton St. Bernard to do the actual work and before it was finished Jack had disappeared, and the £20 with him. No picture of the original Horse exists although Thorne is said to have drawn an artist's impression from the canal bridge to let Pile know what the Horse would look like. By the time of Plenderleath's sketch about 1870 the legs had become rather hairy-heeled, but the head was well preserved for he mentions a mouth and nostril and the ears cut in outline. The general pose seems to be based on the Cherhill horse which is only five miles away.

Nowadays the Alton Barnes Horse looks the perfect creature of spirit, ready to shy on a frosty morning. The slender head and neck and the large round rolling eye, thin ears and long spindly legs give a distinct look of breeding and character. It is about 162 feet long.

Scouring

Sladen reports that during his twelve years in Alton Barnes, from 1856 to 1868, the horse was twice scoured at a cost of a guinea, raised by local subscription. In 1866 fresh chalk was obtained from a pit thoughtlessly opened just above the horse. This has never properly grassed over and can still be seen. Smaller scars below the Horse give it the appearance of walking through clouds.

Since then it has been regularly scoured by local people, Boy Scouts and in 1935, as part of the Jubilee celebrations, by two men paid out of local funds.

Wiltshire
Broad Town Horse

Location
Half a mile N.E. of the village of Broad Town, on the left of the Wooton Bassett-Marlborough road. The site is at forty-five degrees and is on a steep bluff, overlooking the country to the N.W.

Approach
Leave Swindon on A361, the Avebury road. About six miles out of the town turn right along B4041 to Broad Hinton and Broad Town. The Horse lies on the hill to the east of Broad Town.

Best View
When scoured it should be visible for 20 miles from the north. Good view from the Swindon-Bristol railway line, before Wootton Bassett.

History
Plenderleath's date of 1864 is usually accepted as the date when the Horse was cut. It lies within the area of Littletown Farm and is said to have been cut by the farmer, William Simmonds. Simmonds told Plenderleath in 1880 that it was his work and that he had intended eventually to make it larger. However he gave up farming and the chance was lost. This story sounds authentic enough.

However, in the *Morning Post,* 1919, the Curator of the Imperial War Museum told how he, as a boy at school in Wootton Bassett in 1863, had visited it with a friend and spent the day scouring the horse. He adds that an elderly relative of his said it had existed for at least fifty years.

These two stories seem in complete contradiction: another example of how soon memories fade. The only explanation can be that Simmonds himself was in fact only a scourer.

By 1936 the Horse was in a deplorable condition and the lower part of the legs had been lost. It is shown in the usual trotting position but with distinct Hackney action; perhaps Mr. Simmonds was a fancier of this breed.

Wiltshire
Bulford Kiwi

Location

On Beacon Hill, Bulford, on Salisbury Plain. Two miles east of Bulford.

Approach

Leave Amesbury on A303, travelling east. Almost a mile after passing over the railway, take a side road to Bulford on the left. Cross A3028 and Bulford Barracks will be seen ahead. After passing through the group of buildings bear right at the fork and Beacon Hill and the Kiwi will be seen on the right.

Best View

From Bulford Barracks.

History

This bird was cut by New Zealand troops stationed at Sling Camp during the First World War. It covers an acre and a half and is 420 feet long. The letters N.Z. below the beak are 65 feet high and the length of bill 150 feet. At one time the figure was maintained by the Kiwi Polish Company but this responsibility later passed to New Zealand House, who arranged for Mr. R. Paynter of Bulford to care for it. In October 1967 the men of the 1st Battalion Royal Ulster Rifles renovated the bird as a parting gesture before leaving Kiwi Barracks for Gibraltar and photographs appeared in the press of them at work.

Wiltshire
Cherhill Horse

Location

The Horse lies on Cherhill Down, about four miles east of Calne, and near Cherhill village. It is also sometimes called the Oldbury Horse. It lies beneath an ancient earthwork known as Oldbury Castle. The Horse is on a steep slope of forty-five degrees, where the hill falls away from the Castle ramparts. In 1724 Stukeley wrote, "the precipice is altogether inaccessible, falling down in narrow cavities or ribs, as it were the great roots of a tree, and with an odd and tremendous aspect". Modern visitors should not be deterred; Stukeley exaggerated the difficulties.

Approach

Leave Calne on the A4 travelling east in the direction of Marlborough. Cherhill village lies on the road, about three and a half miles from Calne. The Horse is on Cherhill Down, immediately above the village.

Best View

The Horse is visible from at least thirty miles away: some claim to have seen it from Gloucestershire. The best view is from the Bath road. Several tracks lead up to the Horse from Cherhill village.

History

The Horse was cut in 1780, perhaps in imitation of Mr. Gee's work at Westbury. The Reverend W. C. Plenderleath in *On the White Horses of Wiltshire and its Neighbourhood*, 1872, took down the details of its making from an old man, who had often heard the story from those who had been present. Its creator was Dr. Christopher Alsop, of Calne, known as the 'mad doctor' perhaps because of his interest in white horses. Dr. Alsop is supposed to have shouted his instructions from the middle of the village by megaphone to the workmen on Cherhill Down, who planted white flags to mark the outline and as the instructions had to carry over a mile one can presume that Dr. Alsop had a loud voice. The outline from the valley is perfect, with foreshortening eliminated, so this method must have been followed. The Horse is a brisk, eighteenth century, Stubbsian animal, with plenty of what horsey circles call 'impulsion'. From the air, too, the view is particularly striking and lively. It measures nearly 140 feet from nose to tail. According to Plenderleath the usual construction method was used: the turf was removed and pounded chalk rammed in and levelled off. On this steep slope problems of down-flow were found and at one time the chalk was held back by wattles along the lower edge.

A most attractive feature of the Horse was its eye. The inner circle, about four feet in diameter, was filled with old bottles, set with their bases uppermost, which sparkled from a great distance. This information was given to Plenderleath by the nephew of Mr. Angell of Studley. His aunt, Mrs. Angell, had actually provided the bottles from her store-cupboard, but by 1872, souvenir-hunters had stolen them all.

Scouring

This appears to have taken place about every seven years; once more the magic number seven. The Lord of the Manor undertook this duty and chalk was taken from a small pit just over the crest of the hill and let down by truck and windlass. In 1876 one of the workmen nearly lost his life, when the rope broke and the heavily laden truck rushed down the slope. The work is said to have taken six men a fortnight, and it seems to have been real work, with no amusements.

Before the war the owner, Mr. Blackford, tried the experiment of spraying the surface of the Horse with a cement mixture for durability. After wartime camouflage the Horse was restored and resurfaced with a mixture of chalk and cement, but this proved unsatisfactory and Mr. Blackford tells me it was later removed.

Wiltshire
Devizes Horse

Location

This Horse is no longer visible but is supposed to have been cut on the side of Roundway Hill, just below Oliver's Camp, about two miles north of Devizes, on a good site about 600 feet above sea-level.

Local people say that in hot dry summers, a different tone in the grass shows the shape of the horse.

History

The Horse was cut at Whitsuntide, 1845, by the shoemakers of Devizes and was known locally as the Snobs' Horse. But nothing is known of its subsequent history and it seems to have fallen into neglect quite soon.

Wiltshire
Hackpen Horse

Location

On the face of Hackpen Hill, which forms the N.W. limit of Marlborough Downs, on the right of the Wootton Bassett-Marlborough road, where it zig-zags to climb the hill. It is sometimes known as the Broad Hinton or Winterbourne Bassett Horse, after the nearest villages. Ground views are badly distorted as the slope is shallow, although the Horse is on the 750 foot contour line.

Approach

Leave Swindon on the A361. About six miles from the town, almost opposite the turn on the right to the village of Broad Hinton, take a minor road on the left up Fiddlers Hill. The Horse is on the right of a sharp bend a mile and a half up this road.

History

Little is known about the origins of this Horse. It is said to have been cut to commemorate the Coronation of Queen Victoria in 1838 by Henry Eatwell, parish clerk of Broad Hinton and, some say, the local publican.

In shape it belongs to the rest of the Wiltshire group and is really quite similar to the Alton Barnes Horse. It had a docked tail, round eye and two horn-like ears. The hooves are slightly drawn.

When the Horse was first cut the head was banked towards the ears to make it more visible, and the ears are still considerably above turf level. Nothing seems to have been done about the rest of the figure and down-washing has caused banking in the wrong direction. The feet are about 12 inches above the level of the turf. Seen from below the Horse looks more fox-like with swinging gait and long body.

Wiltshire

Laverstock Panda

Location
On the hillside to the left of the A30 Exeter road, about one mile north of Salisbury and just before the A346 turns right to Marlborough and Hungerford and left to Laverstock.
Best View
From the Exeter road. However, the figure is in need of recutting and the features are now faint, although still visible.
History
This figure of a panda's head may perhaps lay claim to the title of England's newest hill figure. The panda and accompanying initials to the right (UCNW) were cut in the early hours of Sunday 26th January 1969 by students from the University College of North Wales, Bangor. Although on common land, the 55 feet by 40 feet figure so alarmed a local farmer that he reported it to the police and consequently the students kept a low profile and did not own up. Reports that the figure was a celebration of the then current meeting at London Zoo between Chi-Chi and the Moscow Zoo panda An-An or, more bizarrely, that it was some kind of homing-in device for Soviet satellites were treated with disdain by UCNW students — the simple explanation was that the panda was the College Rag symbol and the cutting of the figure a Rag Week stunt.

Although hastily cut, the use of turf to represent the black patches round a panda's eyes and ears was convincing. The figure was recut in similar circumstances the following year but, sadly, the current generation of students has not kept up the tradition and the Wiltshire hillside is slowly reclaiming it.

Wiltshire

Marlborough Horse

Location
About one mile S.W. of Marlborough, on Granham Hill. Just above Preshute village.

Approach

Leave Marlborough on the Salisbury road, A345. Half a mile out of the town a track on the right leads up on to Granham Hill. A footpath also leads up from Preshute village, which lies one mile out of Marlborough on the A4, Bath road.

Best View

From the air. The slope on which it lies is only about thirty-five degrees and as no attempt was made to deal with fore-shortening, the view is disappointing from the ground. However, one can be obtained from the Bath road, just short of the Marlborough College Memorial Hall.

History

The Horse was cut in 1804 by a party of boys from Mr. Greasley's Academy in Marlborough. One of the boys, William Canning of Ogbourne St. George, is said to have designed the horse and pegged out the shape on the hill. There seems to have been no particular motive behind the making.

It is a small animal, a mere sixty-two feet long, with a pillow-like appearance. The head suggests a dinosaur, rather than a horse. The ears, shown as one, are pricked and the eye is large and round. The Horse is walking and the tail is docked in the usual way.

Scouring

The boys of the Academy carried out annual scourings until the school closed when Mr. Greasley died, about 1830. The ceremony became one of the school traditions. The horse was then abandoned. However a Marlborough College photograph of about 1860 shows it in the background, so some local interest kept it in existence. This photograph shows only two thick legs, like a Noah's Ark toy, instead of the four visible today. Plenderleath, writing in 1872, noted that the horse was in a bad state but the following year a Captain Read, of Marlborough, who, as a boy had taken part in the cutting (and must have therefore been about 80) had the horse repaired and recut. The whole silhouette became more elegant.

Since then scouring has taken place regularly. It was scoured in 1935 during the Jubilee celebrations, using chalk provided by the land-owner. The local Scout troop dealt with the scouring in 1967. The horse achieves immortality in the Marlborough School Song:

> Ah, then we'll cry, thank God, my lads,
> The Kennett's running still,
> And see, the old White Horse still pads
> Up there on Granham Hill.

Wiltshire
Pewsey Old Horse

Location
The Old Horse was situated on the part of Pewsey Hill, nearest to the village, about a mile away to the south of the Green Drove, which leads to Shepherds Steps. It lay, therefore, a little below and to the right of the Pewsey New Horse. Almost all traces have now gone, although part of it could still be seen about 1938.

History
It is supposed to have been cut about 1785 by Robert Pile, a farmer, of Alton Barnes. Whether this was the same Robert who cut the Alton Barnes Horse in 1812 is a moot point as nearly thirty years separate the two cuttings. Possibly the Alton Barnes Horse was cut by his son of the same name. The last scouring was in 1788 so the cutting was presumably at least a few years earlier. The festivities accompanying the work annoyed the landowner so the figure fell into decay.

A strong local tradition is that the Horse once carried a rider and that in dry weather a faint trace can still be seen. If so, the Pewsey Old Horse, shared this distinction with the Osmington Horse, near Weymouth. On reflection it seems odd that so few of the horses were connected with riders.

Wiltshire
Pewsey New Horse

Location
One and a half miles south of Pewsey, where the road to Everleigh turns to climb the hill and to the left of the road, on the steep slope of Pewsey Hill. It lies somewhat above and to the left of the supposed position of the Pewsey Old Horse and near the 500 foot contour line.

Approach
Leave Pewsey on the A345 travelling south. A quarter of a mile out of the village turn left on the side road to Everleigh. About a mile up this road the Horse will be seen on the left.

Best View
From the wide drove road leading straight to its hillside from the outskirts of Pewsey, where the Pewsey-Amesbury road A345 turns aside from the Downs. Its line is continued by the drove. Another view can be had from the Pewsey-Amesbury road, just south of the village, or from the side road to Everleigh itself.

History

This is the most recent, and perhaps the last, of the Wiltshire Horses. It was designed by George Marples, of Sway, Hampshire, an authority on hill figures. He was investigating the old half-lost Pewsey Horse in the spring of 1937, when suitable commemoration activities for the Coronation of George VI were being discussed. It was suggested that restoration of the Old Horse would be a suitable gesture. Then the question of a new horse was raised and Mr. Marples submitted three designs: a standing horse, a jumping horse with a rider (to continue the tradition that the Pewsey horse had once carried a rider), and a more conventional trotting horse. The last design was chosen. It was pegged out under Mr. Marples' supervision and the actual cutting was done by members of the Pewsey Fire Brigade. The horse is about 65 feet long and 47 feet high. Mr. Marples had himself suffered from difficulty in dating many of the figures so he added the date, 1937, to his own creation.

Scouring

The Horse is on private land. No regular arrangements have been made about scouring but the work has been done as necessary by the children of the local secondary school and by members of Pewsey Vale Young Farmers' Club.

Wiltshire

Regimental Badges at Fovant, Compton Chamberlayne and Sutton Mandeville

Location

Cut in the chalk downs overlooking Fovant, Compton Chamberlayne and Sutton Mandeville, about ten miles west of Salisbury.

Approach

Leave Salisbury on A30 road, travelling west. The badges will be seen on the left along the downs about seven miles after leaving Wilton, near Fovant village. Tracks lead up to the badges.

Best View

From the A30 road.

History

The badges were cut by soldiers stationed in the district during the 1914-18 war and represent the various regiments stationed in the area at the time. The village of Fovant was first used as a training camp and later as a demobilisation centre.

The first badge was cut by the London Rifle Brigade in 1916 in off-duty time. It was so successful that other units quickly followed their example despite the many difficulties encountered in the work. Not only was the hillside steep but the area was in the danger zone of the rifle ranges which were in constant use so the work had to be done early in the morning, from four o'clock to seven o'clock before firing practice began. Sgt. F. Hall of the City of London Rifles who was in charge of the work on his regiment's badge, said that the work took three months to complete and that the badge was 150 feet high. At the end of each morning's work the men would toboggan down the slope on their shovels—an echo of the nineteenth century tobogganing on faggots at Whiteleaf in Buckinghamshire! A number of the many badges and numbers cut have now completely disappeared.

As soon as the troops left at the end of the war the badges became overgrown although some regiments continued to pay local workers for maintenance and the Australian Government took an interest in their badge—the Rising Sun—and in a large kangaroo near it (now overgrown).

By 1939 the maintenance work had to cease. Not only was labour impossible to obtain but it was necessary to camouflage such an excellent aid to enemy aircraft and this was left to nature, which obligingly covered the badges with grass and weeds very quickly. Grazing animals further damaged the outlines. By the end of the war it seemed that the badges might be gone for ever. However the Fovant Home Guard Old Comrades' Association decided to deal with their restoration and in June 1949 twenty-three members of the Association started work on the badges of the 6th Battalion, the London Regt. (6th City of London Rifles) and the London Rifle Brigade. Then the Post Office Rifles badge was cleaned. Early in 1950 it was decided to cut the badge of the Wiltshire Regiment (with the permission of the Colonel of the Regiment)—the badge which the Fovant Home Guard had worn during the war—and in May of that year an informal party was held to inspect the new badge, to which past and present members of the Regiment were invited.

At the same time it was decided to restore the badge of the Australian Expeditionary Force as a gesture of appreciation to the Australian people for the many food parcels received during the war. A local subscription list was opened and the work completed. At the same time a large map of Australia on the downs at Compton Chamberlayne was restored and a flagpole erected in the centre. On Australian Day, January 26th, 1951, an Australian flag was dedicated at the Parish Church and later broken out on the flagpole by members of the Australian forces and of Fovant Home Guard Old Comrades. The flag is now regularly flown on official occasions. Later in 1951 the badge of the Royal Wiltshire Yeomanry was added to the group—perhaps the youngest chalk figure in the world!

Scouring

Maintaining this large group of figures is far from easy and it speaks highly for the enthusiasm of the Old Comrades and other interested local people that they are in such excellent condition today. The badges have all been restored and are now regularly scoured by the local authority.

The badges now to be seen are as follows:
The Royal Wiltshire Regiment
The Wiltshire Regiment
Y.M.C.A.
6th Battalion, The London Regiment (6th City of London Rifles)
Royal Warwickshire Regiment
7th (City of London) Battalion, The London Regiment
Devonshire Regiment
Post Office Rifles
London Rifle Brigade
Australian Imperial Force
Australian Map.

Wiltshire
Westbury Horse

Location

On the steep slope of Bratton Down, about two miles from Westbury and one mile S.W. of the village of Bratton. The slope is about fifty degrees so the Horse can be clearly seen from far away. It faces west, and below stretches Pewsey Vale. Above is Bratton Camp, probably an Iron Age fort, with an earlier long barrow within the fortifications.

Approach

From Devizes take the A360 Amesbury road south, turning right at the crossroads after Littleton Pannell. Follow this road, B3098, for about seven miles to Bratton. The camp is on the left of the road, a mile and a half beyond the village.

Best View

The Horse can be clearly seen from the B3098 road, which runs just below it.

History

The Westbury Horse was not mentioned before the eighteenth century, although the Uffington Horse had already attracted considerable attention. It seems reasonable, therefore, to conclude that it did not exist before then. The first mention is in the Reverend Francis Wise's book, *Further Observations on the White Horse and Other Antiquities in Berkshire,* 1742. He had spoken to local people who said that "it had been wrought within the memory of persons now living or but lately dead". Wise's views were not unchallenged. Gough, the editor of Camden's *Britannia,* looked at the Horse in 1772 and could find no sign of recent cutting. However, as with the other horses, unrecorded events quickly fade from memory and perhaps the work had been quickly forgotten. Gough continued to believe that the Horse was Saxon work.

The Battle of Ethandun in 878 probably took place in the neighbourhood. Some authorities identify the village of Edington, near Bratton, with Ethandun. This faint connection with the events of Alfred's reign has been pounced on by some authorities but it seems little more than a local tradition, which may have started as late as the eighteenth century.

These conjectures apply only to the first Westbury Horse, which was a very different creature to the one we can see today. The earlier Horse, if the sketches are to be believed, was a dachshund-like animal with a long, heavy body and short shapeless legs. Both ears were shown but only one eye, placed oddly below the left ear. Strangest of all was its tail. This curved upwards in a slim reptilian way and had a forked tip. The Horse wore a saddle cloth with two crescent-shaped marks and it was clearly either an antique animal or intended to look so.

Plenderleath, in 1872, believed that the forked tail was strong evidence for antiquity. On many Iron Age coins a crescent moon floated above the figure of the horse. Plenderleath supposed that a similar crescent might have once been placed over the Westbury Horse and through ignorance, was taken to be part of the tail and joined to it. This would make the Horse contemporary with the Uffington Horse.

Six years after Gough formed his theories the first Westbury Horse was destroyed. In 1778 a Mr. Gee, Lord Abingdon's steward, who probably thought himself a judge of horseflesh, remodelled the old Horse, on Stubbsian lines. Perhaps he was irritated every time he set eyes on the bizarre creature.

46

He seems to have been well satisfied with his handiwork but not so his critics. He has since been labelled as a 'vandal', a 'barbarian', a 'wretch' and an 'unimaginative busybody'. The old Horse, said to have faced right, was incorporated within the outline of Gee's Horse and lost for ever.

Little is known of the new Horse until 1853, when restoration took place. In 1873, perhaps as a result of Plenderleath's publicity, it was restored under a local committee at a cost of about £65 and the edge reinforced by stones. In wet weather damage was still caused by water flowing down the outline and gratings were fitted in 1903 to assist drainage. Concrete was added in 1936.

Today the Horse is a well-shaped animal, 182 feet long and 108 feet high. Every feature is marked and the eye is sleepy. The hocks and hooves are well defined and its tail is long, in contrast to the other docked horses of Wiltshire. Nevertheless the impression is mechanical and it is easy to resent Mr. Gee's interference.

Scouring

The only suggestion of merry-making connected with the scouring occurs in Mr. Wise's paper where he speaks of a revel or festival organised by the people of Westbury. Perhaps this was in imitation of the genuine 'pastime' at Uffington. There seems to be no record of this event surviving for long. Scouring has been pure work for the past fifty years and the Horse, together with Bratton Camp, is now in the care of English Heritage.

Yorkshire
Kilburn White Horse

Location

On Roulston Scar, in the Hambleton Hills, seven miles S.E. of Thirsk and near Kilburn village. It lies on a slope of forty degrees just below the Hambleton plateau.

Approach

Leave Pickering on A170, passing through Helmsley and turning left about four miles later at Tom Smith's Cross. Pass through Wass, and fork right at Byland Abbey for Oldstead village. Half a mile outside the village, fork right, and half a mile later a track to the right leads up to the Horse.

Best View

From the south and south-east. At its best it has been seen from Harrogate and from the walls of York, thirty-five miles away.

History

Its origins are clear, which makes a pleasant change from some other figures. It was cut in 1857 and was finished on 4th November. The motivating force was a native of Kilburn, Thomas Taylor, who worked with his brother in their successful grocers' business in London. The shop was noted for its York hams and other delicacies and while travelling in search of these Thomas is said to have been impressed by the Uffington Horse. In fact he may well have attended the scouring described by Thomas Hughes in his novel. He was inspired to plan a similar horse near his native village. It is said that thirty men undertook the work, under the village schoolmaster, and that six tons of lime were used for white-washing. Taylor paid for the maintenance in his lifetime and public subscription dealt with the cost later. The Ecclesiastical Commissioners, as the landowners, contributed through their agent. No celebrations accompanied the work.

It is a large standing animal, only slightly shorter than the Uffington Horse with horn-like ears, blurred feet and a large round eye. It measures 314 feet long and 228 feet high and the eye is large enough to allow twenty people to sit upon it. The site is exposed and a hailstorm in 1896 is said to have almost destroyed it.

ACKNOWLEDGEMENTS

The National Trust and their Area agents; Col. H. R. Grace, O.B.E., D.L., J.P.; Clerk of the Council, Pewsey R.D.C.; Kiwi Polish Company; Sussex Archaeological Society; The Curator, County Museum, Aylesbury; Birmingham Public Libraries; Weymouth Public Library; Whipsnade Zoo; K. Carrdus, Esq., of Banbury; Dr H. H. Glasscock; Miss E. S. Smyth of Wye College; Roger Parker-Jervis, Esq., Agent to the Hampden Settlement; D. G. Blackford, Esq., of Cherhill; The Curator, The Museum, Devizes; The Town Clerk, Marlborough Borough Council; Fovant Badges Society.

The lines from *Ballad of the White Horse* by G. K. Chesterton from *Collected Poems* are included by kind permission of Miss D. E. Collins and Methuen & Co. Ltd. Diagrams in the text are reproduced from *White Horses and other Hill Figures* by kind permission of M. Marples, Esq.

The publishers acknowledge the assistance of Fiona Marsden, Curator of the Sussex Archaeological Society, and Mr Dave Reeder for their assistance in the preparation of the third edition.